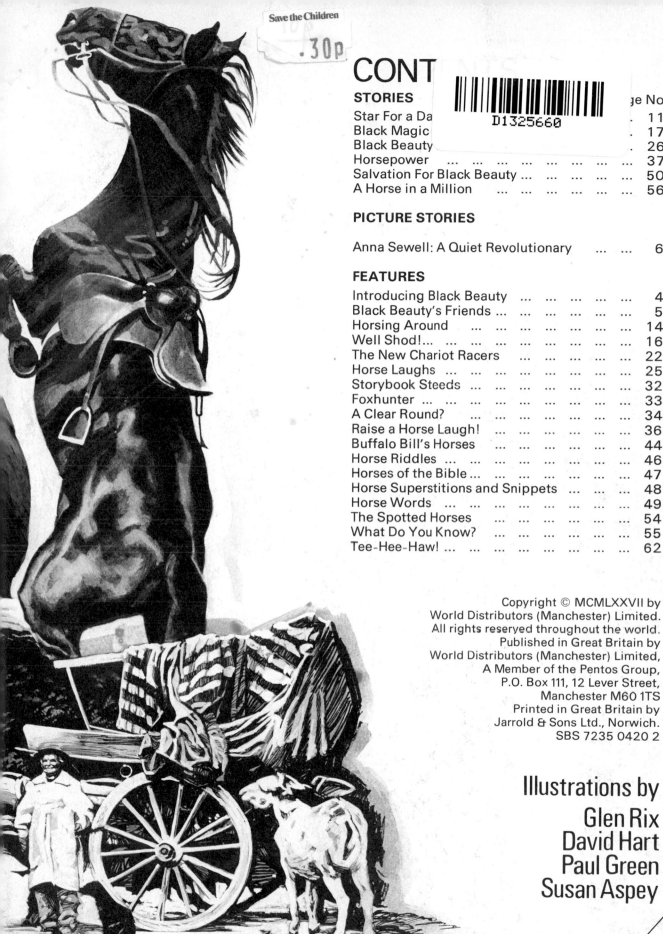

D1325660

CONT[ENTS]

Copyright © MCMLXXVII by
World Distributors (Manchester) Limited.
All rights reserved throughout the world.
Published in Great Britain by
World Distributors (Manchester) Limited,
A Member of the Pentos Group,
P.O. Box 111, 12 Lever Street,
Manchester M60 1TS
Printed in Great Britain by
Jarrold & Sons Ltd., Norwich.
SBS 7235 0420 2

Illustrations by

Glen Rix
David Hart
Paul Green
Susan Aspey

£1·35

Introducing Black Beauty

During the nineteenth century many horses were cruelly treated by their owners, and in order to draw attention to their plight, Anna Sewell, who loved horses, wrote a story about the adventures of one horse. She called her book *Black Beauty* and it soon became a bestseller.

In the book we follow Black Beauty's life, from his early days in a pleasant meadow with his mother, through his time at Birtwick Park with Squire Gordon and kind John Manley, to the harsher days when he became a 'job' horse and a cab horse until happier times came along again and he became a small boy's pet horse.

Beauty introduces us to his old horse friends, Merrylegs, Ginger and the old war horse Captain, as well as to his human friends, Mr Blomefield the vicar, little Joe Green, Jerry Barker and old Farmer Thoroughgood.

Anna Sewell wrote this classic horse story in 1877, over a hundred years ago, and it is still as popular today as ever. In our annual are several more adventures which could have befallen Black Beauty on his travels.

We hope that you will enjoy reading all about the adventures of this courageous and intelligent horse who does all he can to help anyone in distress whom he meets on his travels, for Black Beauty is one of the best known and best loved fictional animals in the world.

Black Beauty's friends

Black Beauty met many other horses on his travels and made friends with them. Among the horses were:

Merrylegs

was a handsome little grey pony that Beauty met when he went to live at Birtwick Park. He was a little on the fat side, but a cheerful, plucky little fellow, good-tempered and a favourite with everyone.

Ginger

who was a tall chestnut mare with a long handsome neck. She got on well with Black Beauty, but she once snapped at a groom and made his arm bleed. She told Beauty she had once been very badly treated by a man called Samson, and had come to distrust men since that day. Sad to say, Beauty met his old friend much later and found her being mistreated once again, and this resulted in Ginger getting a bad cough which finally killed her.

Sir Oliver

was an old brown hunter, now long past an active working life, but still a great favourite with the Squire, who sometimes let Sir Oliver do a little light carting work on the estate. Sir Oliver hated blinkers on a horse and said that they did more harm than good.

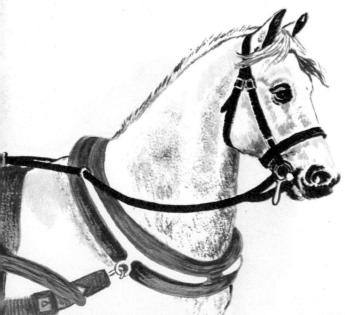

Captain

became a friend of Beauty during his days as a cab horse. He was a tall, white, large-boned animal, but he was highly-bred, fine mannered and a noble old horse who in his youth had belonged to a Cavalry officer. Captain had seen service in the Crimean War with his master.

Anna Sewell: A Quiet Revolutionary

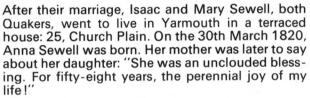

It is not given to us all to influence society, but Anna Sewell, through her sympathetic novel *Black Beauty*, made Victorians aware of the over-working and ill-treatment of horses at that time and so became their champion, spokeswoman and saviour. Her revelations of the cruelty and torture of the bearing-rein really managed to make the smug sit up and take notice!

After their marriage, Isaac and Mary Sewell, both Quakers, went to live in Yarmouth in a terraced house: 25, Church Plain. On the 30th March 1820, Anna Sewell was born. Her mother was later to say about her daughter: "She was an unclouded blessing. For fifty-eight years, the perennial joy of my life!"

Soon after their little girl was born, the Sewells decided to move to a small house in Camomile Street, off Bishopsgate, London, and there to establish a small business — a drapery shop specialising in Quaker attire.

Mary, so used to the countryside of Buxton where she had spent her childhood, loathed London, particularly the poverty she found there. Agricultural labourers and their families had moved there, due to the Industrial Revolution, and now lived in unbelievably crowded and unhealthy conditions. Mary Sewell made it her job to help these families whenever she could, particularly the children.

The shop was not a success and the reason was that not far away there was another Quaker drapery, much bigger, where business was thriving. To help, Mary Sewell used to sew garments during the day, which were sold in their little shop.

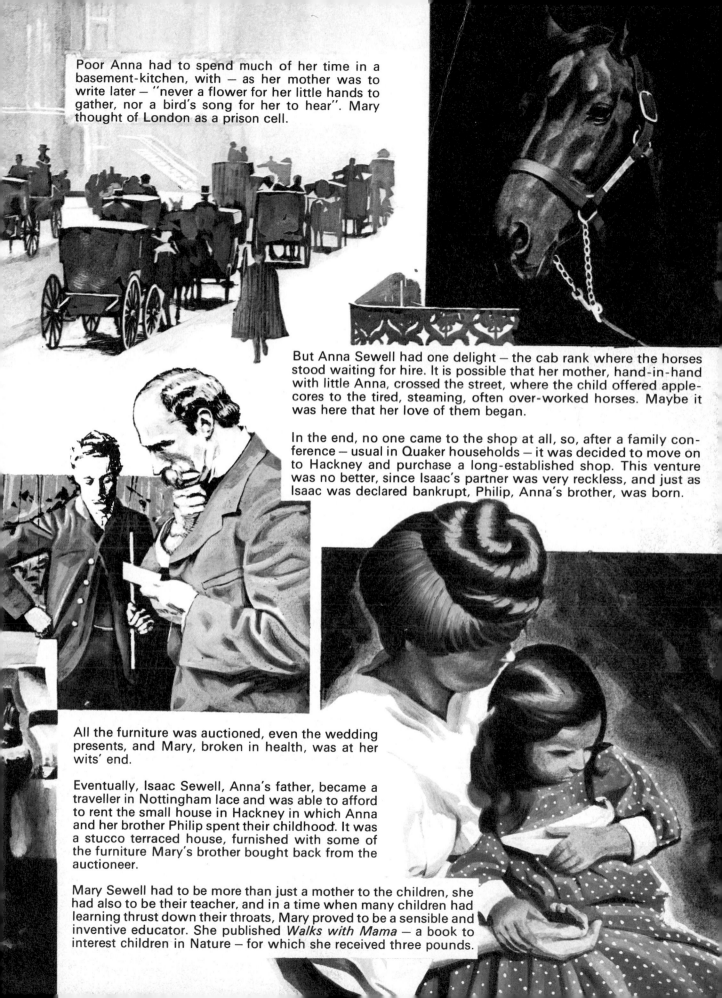

Poor Anna had to spend much of her time in a basement-kitchen, with — as her mother was to write later — "never a flower for her little hands to gather, nor a bird's song for her to hear". Mary thought of London as a prison cell.

But Anna Sewell had one delight — the cab rank where the horses stood waiting for hire. It is possible that her mother, hand-in-hand with little Anna, crossed the street, where the child offered apple-cores to the tired, steaming, often over-worked horses. Maybe it was here that her love of them began.

In the end, no one came to the shop at all, so, after a family conference — usual in Quaker households — it was decided to move on to Hackney and purchase a long-established shop. This venture was no better, since Isaac's partner was very reckless, and just as Isaac was declared bankrupt, Philip, Anna's brother, was born.

All the furniture was auctioned, even the wedding presents, and Mary, broken in health, was at her wits' end.

Eventually, Isaac Sewell, Anna's father, became a traveller in Nottingham lace and was able to afford to rent the small house in Hackney in which Anna and her brother Philip spent their childhood. It was a stucco terraced house, furnished with some of the furniture Mary's brother bought back from the auctioneer.

Mary Sewell had to be more than just a mother to the children, she had also to be their teacher, and in a time when many children had learning thrust down their throats, Mary proved to be a sensible and inventive educator. She published *Walks with Mama* — a book to interest children in Nature — for which she received three pounds.

Mary Sewell was influenced in her teaching by Richard and Maria Edgeworth — disciples of Rousseau — who believed that children should be brought up to be self-reliant and independent. However, disobedience was punished, and play carefully supervised, as were the children's lessons.

The children learned that they should be kind to animals and the story is told of how, on one occasion, Anna reacted strongly to a man who had killed a blackbird, saying: "Thee cruel man, thee shan't have it at all!" — the man having knocked on the door of their house demanding the bird.

The children often spent their summers with their grandfather on his farm at Buxton, and the journeys there by stagecoach must have been exciting. They thought Buxton a Paradise and Anna loved harvest-time and seeing the great Suffolk Punches led out into the yard to be harnessed.

But not far away was Uncle Wright and his big house. He had a stable and it was there Anna learned to ride: at first the pony from her aunt's chaise and later Balaam, an excellently mannered horse who was gentle and used to being ridden side-saddle.

She was also taught to drive, probably by her Aunt. Aunt Wright was a marvellous woman, fond of natural history and a great storyteller. She published *The Observing Eye* in 1850, to instruct children in the love of natural things. Queen Victoria read it and found it "quite suitable for the royal nursery!"

Later, we hear of Philip's engagement to Sarah Woods, a Quaker girl from Tottenham, but we hear of no romance for poor Anna! Anna was lame, you see, and this was soon to be a handicap to her not only physically, but psychologically.

As a young woman, Anna began to shuttle between one religion and another, just as her mother was to do, and from time to time, she suffered agonies of spiritual loneliness, and a terrible doubt about whether she had faith at all.

Between 1845 and 1858, the Sewells moved about Sussex restlessly. At first they were in a house at Lancing, and it was about this time that a pony and trap was bought, much to Anna's delight. Margaret Sewell, Anna's niece, has said that Anna was an excellent driver who could convey her wishes to horses with the minimum of effort.

It was at Lancing that Anna began to complain of lack of energy, of a weak back and lack of concentration. And though gifted in so many ways — in how to arrange a vase of flowers, for instance, in how to express something clearly and succinctly — her niece has described the terrible times when Anna would be unable to concentrate for more than a few minutes together.

Part of the trouble may have been her separation from her brother Philip, with whom she was extremely close; he was now a civil engineer and was working abroad. But her mother wrote about Anna: "Her own mind was always a storehouse of refreshment to herself; it was a rich garden which circumstances never allowed to be fully cultivated."

The first spa Anna Sewell visited was Marienbad in Czechoslovakia, then Bohemia, but later she went to Matlock and was lucky enough to meet the poet Tennyson, of whose poetry she was extremely fond. It is considered likely that they met at Umberslade Hall, an eighteenth century mansion, in 1847.

Between 1864–67 the Sewells moved to Bath, but lived in Norwich between the years 1867–77. The White House, 125 Spixworth Road, three miles north of Norwich, still stands: and the room in which *Black Beauty* was written has changed little, except for the disappearance of the balcony outside.

Philip advised Anna on the technical details of the manuscript of *Black Beauty* and his visits to the White House were looked forward to immensely. However, Anna often leant out of the window to carry on instructive conversations with the cabmen in the street and so was able to learn the idioms of their speech and to gain some insight into their natures.

When the manuscript was completed, Mary Sewell took it along to the publishers Jarrolds at their London office in Paternoster Row. The manager there, a Mr Tillyer, offered £20 for the copyright of the book. The book was published on 24th November 1877.

It is estimated that over thirty million copies of *Black Beauty* have been sold to date. It has been filmed and televised and continues to be probably the best animal story ever written. It was not specifically written for children but, as stated, to arouse sympathy for the horses of the Victorian era, often cruelly treated.

Anna Sewell died towards the end of April 1878, looked after by her beloved mother. She was buried in the cemetery close to the Quaker Meeting House at Lammas where her parents were married. She was 58 years old.

STAR FOR A DAY

It was a crisp, bright autumn morning, and the red and russet leaves crunched and crackled under the horses' hooves as they galloped and cantered along London's Rotten Row. Black Beauty rode with his new master, James Smythe, and James's sister Sarah. Beauty was happy in his new home at the Smythe house, for although James was only twelve years old he was a proficient horseman and a very keen rider.

As James and Black Beauty rounded a corner on the Row, a very strange sight greeted them. It was so strange that James and Sarah reined in their mounts and sat quite still, looking down along the tree-lined path. An unusual group of riders were coming into view. . . .

At their head rode a tall, imposing man with long hair and a flowing beard. He was wearing suede tasselled trousers and shirt, high-heeled boots with gleaming spurs and a large cowboy

hat. The men riding with him wore similar clothes, with wide-brimmed hats and high boots in tooled leather, rather like the saddles their horses wore. They were an impressive sight, but looked so out of place in the middle of London that James and Sarah gaped rudely as they approached.

As the group drew level, the man at their head reined in his horse and lifted his large stetson hat.

"Pleased to make your acquaintance," the man said to James and Sarah, in an accent that James thought was probably American. "Couldn't help noticing that that's a mighty fine horse you're riding, young man."

James was lost for words, but he felt very proud that this imposing stranger had stopped just to remark on Black Beauty. "Thank you, er, sir," James stuttered. "His name is Black Beauty, and my father bought him for my birthday."

"Name suits him just fine," said the stranger,

11

stroking Beauty's head and ears just the way he liked it. "He's intelligent, too?"

"Oh, yes!" said James, forgetting his shyness. "Beauty can do almost anything I ask him to. He seems to know just what I want him to do – almost before I know I want to do it myself!"

"Yeah, he sure is a fine and dandy horse," said the stranger. "Well, I guess we'd best be on our way. Good day to you."

Then, just as James and Sarah were about to ride off down the Row, the man called out to them. "Say," he said, "would you two youngsters like to have some tickets for my show tonight? Be glad if you could come along." The man thrust some tickets into James's hand, and the riders galloped off.

James watched until the riders were out of sight, almost forgetting the tickets in his hand. When he looked at them he gasped. "Wow!" he said at last. "I just don't believe it!"

"Believe what?" asked Sarah, leaning out of her saddle to look at the tickets. "What are the tickets for? Let me see!"

"Oh, you won't believe it, Sarah," said James. "Do you know who that man is? He's Buffalo Bill, the real Buffalo Bill – and these are four tickets for his Wild West Show tonight!"

"That's marvellous!" said Sarah. "We should have recognised him from the posters that have been pasted everywhere. Do you think Father will take us?"

"I hope so," said James, turning Beauty back the way they had ridden. "Let's go and find out!"

That evening the horses were harnessed to the Smythe carriage, and the whole family drove out in the twilight to watch the Wild West Show. When the attendant saw their tickets he ushered James and Sarah and their parents into special seats reserved for them near the entrance to the arena. There they could watch the preparations and saddling of the horses as well as the show itself.

Just before the show began, James saw Buffalo Bill himself in the saddling enclosure, and waved. Bill walked over and said hello to James and his parents, and was just telling them what was about to happen in the show when he was interrupted by one of his men.

"Sorry to butt in, Bill," said the man, "but it's Old Charlie. He's gone lame. I've had a look at him, and I think he'll be OK in a coupla days, but you won't be able to ride him tonight."

Buffalo Bill clapped his hand to his forehead. "And Silver's lame too! What am I gonna do, Jack?"

"I dunno," said the helper. "You're just gonna have to find another horse to ride in the finale, I guess."

Bill turned to James and his parents. "I guess I'd better explain to you folks," he said. "Old Charlie is my horse – and what a horse he is. I ride him in all the displays in the show, and now he's lame. So's my second horse, Silver. Looks like there ain't gonna be no show tonight, not unless I find me a new horse – fast."

A smile crept across James's face. "Well, there's Black Beauty, if . . ."

"Say, you might have something there," said Buffalo Bill. "You said he was an intelligent horse, and he sure looks fine enough to appear in the show. Do you think he could stay calm? Remember, there'll be a lot of shooting and shouting going on in the attack on the stage coach."

"Oh, I'm sure he could," said James. "Black Beauty used to be a cab horse, and he's used to noise and bustle. Isn't he, Father?"

Mr Smythe nodded. "Yes, Mr . . . er . . . Bill, Black Beauty is a very calm, steady horse. And if you're sure you want to use him in the show, please do."

Buffalo Bill smiled. "Well, that's settled then," he said. "Come on, James. Show me where this horse of yours is, and we'll get him saddled up!"

When James returned to his seat he was so excited that he could hardly concentrate on the Wild West Show. He watched Annie Oakley's sharp-shooting displays, and the bronco-busters, and Sitting Bull riding his fine Indian pony, but what he was really waiting for was the finale of the show, when Buffalo Bill was to ride *his* horse, Black Beauty.

At last the moment arrived, and the stage coach entered the ring, pulled by four fine horses. Then, as the crowd watched, (pretend) hostile Indians raced after it, ready for the attack. Dud bullets whistled through the air, smoke swirled around the arena, and the air was full of the shouts and war cries of the Indians, who caught up with and circled the stage coach, ready for the final attack. . . .

Then, to a great roar from the crowded spectators, into the ring rode Buffalo Bill on Black Beauty, who was decked out in silver-ornamented saddle and bridle, his mane flowing as he carried Buffalo Bill at lightning speed across the arena. The crowd roared and cheered as Buffalo Bill, guns thundering, rescued the stage coach, drove off the Indians, and rode triumphantly around the ring.

And no one in the audience cheered and clapped louder than James and his family as Black Beauty rode proudly out of the arena. Tomorrow he'd be back riding along Rotten Row with James – but for that night he was the star of Buffalo Bill's Wild West Show.

HORSING AROUND

"He's a fine horse, but something tells me the jockey lacks experience."

"Is this the first fox hunt you've been on?"

"Henry doesn't seem to be eating a lot these days."

"I hear the water-jump's pretty stiff here." "He works in a pet-shop when he's not riding."

"Right then, it's agreed.
We go neck and neck for the whole race,
then stop dead just before the winning post."

"He's done much better since he saw *Jaws*."

"Personally, I wouldn't be seen
dead in pyjamas like that."

"It says number 12 acts best in wet weather."

Whizzo the talking horse
— ask him anything

"He's not so clever really,
the dog tells him all the answers."

"This fox is one of the craftiest
in the country."

WELL SHOD!

Wild horses and ponies are able to roam the moorlands without any protection for their feet, but for domestic horses it is a very different matter. Horses kept for riding and working may be expected to be on their feet for many hours a day, and may have to travel over a wide variety of surfaces — stones, fields, hard roads and even sand. For this reason their feet need protection, and this is given in the form of the familiar horseshoe.

Long Ago . . .

Shoeing horses isn't a modern idea. Horses have been fitted with some form of foot protection for over 2,000 years. The ancient Greeks fitted their horses with hippo-sandals, held onto the hoof by leather thonging. The Japanese and ancient Egyptians used another form of protection — straw sandals, which were tied to the hoof with tight knots. But this was not a very reliable method, as the straw wore through very quickly, and the sandals often slipped off.

It was the ancient Romans who vastly improved the idea. They realised that iron shoes, fitted on with nails, were the most secure form of protection, and it is this method, with certain modifications, which is still in use today.

As man used horses more and more, both for transport and in the fields, the method of shoeing developed into a skilled craft, and every village had its own forge and blacksmith. There each horse would be individually fitted with new shoes by the skilled blacksmith.

And Today . . .

But today a village smithy is a rare thing, and the modern trend is not for the horse to visit the blacksmith, but for the blacksmith to visit the horse. This presents problems, however, for shoes cannot be made to fit each individual horse.

The blacksmith might take shoes along with him, and try to fit them cold, but this would not give the good, close fit that is so important. So nowadays many blacksmiths carry a portable forge with them, so that they can make the shoes on the spot.

BLACK MAGIC

The early morning mist still lingered over the New Forest, but soon the sun would drive the last few patches away. Across the fields the first warm rays caught the thatched roof of Rose Cottage, and glinted on the leaded windows.

Inside, Ellen and Hannah Tozer were preparing breakfast. They were in more of a hurry than usual, because a letter had arrived, and it was a rule with them that they did not open letters until breakfast was over. As sisters, they couldn't have looked less alike, for Ellen was tall, slim and placid, while Hannah was short, plump and vivacious. However, for all that they were very close, and managed to live together without any of the arguments that might have arisen between two people with the same temperament.

Today it was Ellen's turn to read the letter, and as soon as they finished eating, she opened it carefully with the paper knife.

Hannah could barely contain her impatience, but she sat quietly until her sister looked up. "It's from Percy," she said. (Percy was their elder brother.) "He asks if we will look after Laura until his own children recover from scarlet fever. You know how sickly she is, and he is afraid that she will catch the fever if she stays in London."

Laura was the only child of their younger brother, Sidney, so tragically killed with his young wife in a fire the year before. Although she had been rescued, she was in such a state of shock that she had never spoken a word since, although her Aunt Martha and Uncle Percy had tried their best to help her. They had been happy to bring Laura into their home, but they had three of their own children, and couldn't spend as much time with the sad little girl as they would have liked.

As for Laura, she shrank from the company of her boisterous cousins and spent most of her time on her own, reading or sketching. She had never been seen to cry since her parents' death, and her aunt and uncle were of the opinion that this was part of the trouble. Doctors had tried to make her speak, but all had failed, and it was generally agreed that Laura would be dumb for the rest of her life.

"That poor child," said Hannah, shaking her head sadly. "Does Percy say when she will be coming?"

"According to this, she should be here to-morrow," said Ellen. "He is anxious to get her out of the house as soon as possible, so we had better get the little front room ready today."

The London coach arrived at twelve the next day, and the two sisters walked into the village to meet it. While the coachman lifted the bags down, Ellen helped Laura down from the coach.

Hannah's eyes filled with tears at the sight of the pathetic little figure, and she hugged her warmly.

Although she was ten years old, the child was so small and thin that she could have been taken for seven or eight. Her face was alarmingly pale, and her eyes were ringed with shadows. Hannah was afraid that she had already contracted scarlet fever, but Ellen assured her that there was nothing wrong that country air and wholesome food wouldn't cure.

They reached the cottage, and Ellen took Laura up to see her room. Although it was small it was bright and cheerful, with a patchwork quilt, a gaily coloured rug, and a pink geranium on the windowsill. "I sleep in the next room, and you have only to knock on the wall if you want me during the night," said Ellen.

That night, Laura went to bed early, but she was overtired and couldn't sleep. Kneeling on the bed, she rested her arms on the windowsill and stared out into the twilight. In the distance she could just make out the dim shape of the New Forest, while down below was the small paddock and stable that had once housed Prince, a big black horse who had died when Laura was very small. One of her few memories of Prince was the feel of his warm breath on her hand when she fed him a piece of apple.

Tomorrow she would go exploring in the forest, and maybe do some sketching while she was there. She realised that she was shivering, and she snuggled down under the patchwork quilt. Within minutes she was fast asleep, dreaming of black horses and apples.

The next morning Ellen had some shopping to do, so Hannah asked Laura what she would like to do. The little girl pointed out of the window at the forest, and then picked up her sketch book.

"Ah," said Hannah, "you want to go for a walk. Very well. I'll just tell your Aunt Ellen where we'll be."

As they crossed the fields, Hannah kept up a flow of lively chatter, but although Laura smiled politely every so often, her stiff little face never relaxed.

By the time they reached the New Forest, Hannah was quite breathless. She told Laura that she would sit down and rest for a while. "You do some sketching, and we'll go exploring when I get my breath back," she said.

Laura wandered off into the forest, and found a mossy place where she could sit and watch the birds as they swooped above her head. She liked it here because it was quiet, and she could sit without anyone coming and telling her to play, as her cousins would have done. She opened her sketch book to draw a squirrel that had appeared

on a branch, but before she could begin, there was a rustling sound behind her.

It was coming her way, and she sat very still, hoping that whoever it was would pass her by. Suddenly a horse crashed through the bushes. A big black horse, just like Prince. He seemed to stagger, as if his legs couldn't bear his weight, and she could see that he was trembling. He seemed to sense that she was there, for he stood facing her, shaking his head, and whinnying softly.

"He wants me to help him," she thought. "He's ill, and he's asking me to help him."

Black Beauty was indeed very ill. He had been wandering through the New Forest for several days, lost, hungry, and weak from the fever that made him hot, and yet made him shiver too. For most of the morning he had lain in the mossy shade, but at last his raging thirst had sent him looking for water, and that was when he saw Laura.

Meanwhile, the warm sun and exercise had made Hannah drowsy, and she was just nodding off as Laura ran up to her. She brought her head up with a start as Laura shook her arm.

"Good gracious, child, whatever's the matter?" she said. "Have you found something? Oh, I see, you want me to follow you."

Laura nodded vigorously, and ran off again. Hannah followed as fast as she could, thinking that the child must want to show her a flower or a bird.

She finally caught up with her, and gasped, "Now, what did you want to show me? Oh, a horse! And he's in a bad way too, the poor thing!"

She approached him slowly, thinking that he might run away, but Beauty stood quite still.

"See how thin he is," said Hannah. "He must not belong to anyone round here. I think we should take him home, don't you?" Laura nodded again, and Hannah was pleased to see that her face had lost that tense look, and was almost animated. "Come on, my boy, easy does it."

They led Beauty slowly back to the cottage.

As soon as Ellen saw the sick horse she said, "Take him to the stable and make him comfortable. I'll go for the vet."

Laura was sent for a blanket, and soon Beauty was wrapped up warmly.

The vet did what he could to make him comfortable, and told the sisters that now it was up to them. "The fever will probably get worse," he said, "but if he pulls through that, he'll be fine."

They brought straw for the stable, and Beauty lay down. Laura gently stroked his nose, and the warm breath caressed her hand.

"Please get better," she thought. "I'll look after you, I promise, and then you'll be strong and beautiful again."

For the first time since her parents' death she forgot her own misery, and all her sympathies were transferred to the horse.

Although Ellen and Hannah were busy looking after Beauty, they noticed the change in Laura, and let her help as often as she wanted to. The little girl looked almost happy as she sat down for tea, and Ellen hoped for her sake that the horse would pull through.

The fever raged for twenty-four hours, and there was little they could do but wait. Poor Black Beauty! His eyes were glazed, and he lay shivering in the straw, although he was very hot, and would shake off the rug if they tried to wrap him up.

On the second day, Ellen sent Laura out to the stable with Beauty's medicine. Once again the rug had been tossed onto the floor, and as she picked it up, Laura noticed how still Beauty was.

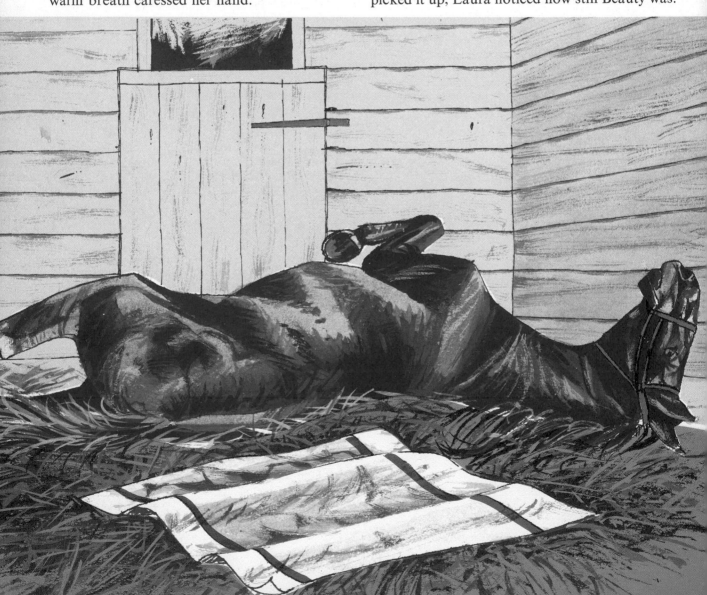

eyes opened wide in delight. The soft warm breath came rhythmically and Ellen smiled. "He's asleep at last," she said, "and that means that he's going to get well." Her own eyes were rather misty, and she wiped them on her shawl.

Suddenly she sat bolt upright. "Laura!" she said. "You spoke! By all that's wonderful, you actually spoke!"

Laura smiled happily. "The magic that made my horse better has made me better too," she said simply.

Ellen hugged her tightly, and silently thanked Beauty for bringing about this miracle. "He is obviously a very special horse," she said, "and we are very lucky to have met him, aren't we?" As she spoke they heard Hannah calling to them from the cottage.

"Let's go and tell your aunt Hannah the good news," said Ellen, "and find a tasty treat for Beauty. He certainly deserves it!"

Beauty stirred, and opened his eyes.

"I think he heard that!" laughed Laura.

His eyes were closed, and he was no longer shaking. She knelt beside him and touched his side. It was cold.

"He can't be dead!" she thought. "He mustn't be dead after I've tried so hard to make him better!" Hot tears ran down her cheeks, the first since her parents' death, and she ran blindly across the yard.

Ellen was on her way to pick some blackberries, and Laura flung herself into her arms. "He's dead!" she sobbed. "My beautiful horse is dead, and I so wanted him to get better! Why do all the things I love have to die?"

Without a word, Ellen hurried to the stable. She knelt over the body of Black Beauty and put her hand on his face.

"Come here," she said gently as Laura hung back. "Put your hand here."

Laura put her hand on Beauty's nose, and her

THE NEW CHARIOT RACERS

Bigger and stronger than the ass, faster than the ox and more amenable to training than either, the horse has held a special place in man's affections ever since our ancestors gave up their nomadic existences as hunters and took to farming and herding to provide for themselves. From the moment one of the more athletic of our ancestors first leapt on his back, the horse's destiny has been so strongly linked to man's that there are virtually no truly wild horses left on earth. There are horses of all shapes and sizes, bred for all manner of tasks from pulling coal down pits to racing at Ascot, that would never have existed if man hadn't found the horse such a useful and fascinating animal.

One of the first things man taught the horse was how to pull things, and it wasn't long after this that they began racing with small buggies behind. It has often been argued that the sport of racing wheeled vehicles pulled by horses is older than that of racing on a horse's back,

and it is a fact that chariot racing preceded horse racing in the Olympic games by two hundred years. There was chariot racing in Mesopotamia five thousand years ago, but whichever sport came first, both have survived to this day.

The modern equivalent of chariot racing is harness racing with Standardbred horses, a sport that is extremely popular in America and which is beginning to break new ground in Britain. Harness racing has a long and varied history, from the Roman amphitheatres via English country lanes to the main strip in Harlem, but it was the introduction of Standardbred horses that set harness racing on its way to the position it occupies today, only marginally less popular than Thoroughbred horse racing.

Standardbred horses are horses that are bred to cover a mile inside a certain time limit. This limit has come down ever since harness racing first accepted these standards, until now the required time is two

and a half minutes.

Harness racing has been slow to gain popularity in England. In Germany, France, Italy, Holland, Russia, Belgium, Australia and Japan it is thriving. It has been popular in America for more than two hundred years, but it was only in September 1940, when night harness racing was introduced in the floodlit Roosevelt Raceway, that it really began to take off. The Americans, noticing how the 4,500 crowd enjoyed it, used their unequalled knowledge of promotion to turn it into the multi-million dollar business it is today, attracting more than twenty-five million spectators last year. Harness racing centres were set up throughout the United States and Canada, some costing almost 10,000,000 dollars to build. The days of racing round converted abandoned motor-racing circuits were over. Harness racing was here to stay.

Along with the increase in gates came an increase in prize money and stud fees. As the competition hotted up, the equipment became more and more sophisticated. Modern buggies, known as sulkies, are almost free of friction, so that the weight of the driver is far less important than that of a jockey. Skill is the important thing and it is well rewarded. As far back as 1964, Stanley Dancer became the first man to top a million dollars in winnings in a single season.

Because the weight of the driver is not so important, there are far more owner/drivers than owner/jockeys in racing. But before an owner can line up at the start he must decide whether to train his horse as a trotter, a pacer or both.

Most Standardbred horses are born with an aptitude for either pacing or trotting. A few are double-gaited. When trotting, the front and rear legs of opposite sides of the horse move in the same direction at the same time. When pacing, the front and back legs of the same side move together. Pacers are marginally quicker over a mile,

due to their ability to get away from the start faster than a trotter. Speed when running is virtually the same.

BEFORE THE RACE

Both pacing and trotting are highly mannered, very correct gaits that require patient handling and a lot of training. When a horse is travelling at full speed its natural gait is the gallop — when pacing and trotting they must learn to extend themselves within the confines of the two styles. This is one of the reasons the pre-race tactics of flat racers and harness racers are so different. The most exercise a Thoroughbred horse can expect immediately before a race is a pipe-opening gallop down to the start. Standardbred horses are exercised for two hours before the start, with the trainer splitting his programme into three distinct parts.

Firstly, the Standardbred horse jogs slowly round the track in the opposite direction to that which he will be running.

He is fitted with a minimal harness, and after covering about two and a half miles is turned round and taken back at a faster speed. He goes back to the paddock, where he is sponged down. After half an hour he practises a few starts and then does a mile at a brisk pace. He then goes back to the paddock where he is sponged down again. Then, about thirty minutes before the race is due to be run, the horse is given his final preparation — a spin round the track at a pace only a few seconds slower than he will be trying for in the actual race. This elaborate routine is essential to loosen up the horse so that he will perform to the best of his abilities.

In the race itself, much depends on the skill and experience of the driver. It is an accepted fact in harness racing that a driver who has more than two opportunities to extend his horse fully is very lucky indeed. The secret is to time these short bursts to give the horse and driver the maximum advantage. Different horses like to race in

different ways, and a reinsman must know the whims of his horse if he is to be first past the post.

HEROES OF THE SPORT

Like all popular sports, harness racing has its legends and heroes. One such hero was Hambletonian 10, to whom nearly ninety per cent of today's Standardbred horses can be traced. In his twenty-four year career at stud he sired more than thirteen hundred foals, of which forty cracked the two-and-a-half minute barrier for the mile, a time which in those days of slow tracks and heavy-wheeled sulkies, was equivalent to a man running a four-minute mile today.

In 1895 a new kind of sulky was introduced, with small pneumatic tyred wheels and a low seat, similar to the kind used today. This, and the introduction of hopples, to stop horses breaking their stride, led to the first two-minute mile in 1897. Harness racing had won a new

lease of life — all that it needed was a new champion. In Dan Patch, perhaps the greatest pacer ever, it got one.

Dan Patch broke the two-minute mile more than thirty times, breaking the record as a seven, eight and nine-year-old. His 1906 time of $1:55\frac{1}{4}$ stood for thirty-three years and today it is within seconds of the existing world record. When you remember that present day tracks and equipment are much better than they were in those days you can understand just how fast he was.

Then Henry Ford began his campaign to put America on wheels, and harness racing went into decline. With less and less harness horses needed for travel, there were less and less bred, less and less for racing. By the start of the Second World War, harness racing was reduced to novelty status at country fairs.

But night racing changed all that and with the new interest came a new kind of hero. Stanley Dancer, George Sholty, Robert Farrington and Del Insko are a new breed of American hero who can be seen most nights on

the harness racing tracks. They are men of experience and judgement, able to handle the most fractious of the usually mild-mannered Standardbreds, able to find gaps in the field and coax out the speed to go through them, able to conjure an extra yard from their horses in a blanket finish. Age is no barrier to the harness driver, as Frank Ervin proved with his twenty-four successive wins and 173,298 dollars winnings from driving Bret Hanover in 1964.

A harness racing meeting in Blackburn might seem un-glamorous when compared to Grand Circuit meetings in Phoenix or New York, and it's true that the American harness racing scene is much more vital and prosperous than it is here. But the sport in this country is definitely growing, slowly and steadily attracting a wider audience, ready to pay for the thrills and excitement of a night at the track. Who knows, maybe one day there will be harness racing in front of 100,000 screaming fans at Wembley Stadium? Let's hope so.

Horse Laughs

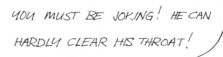

Ann: Why are horses so hard to get on with?
Sam: I don't know.
Ann: Because they always say *neigh*, of course!

Tom was riding through the park one day on his horse, Fella, when they met a large dog.

"Hello there," said the dog.

"Hello there," said Tom, and he rode on through the park.

"That's a very strange thing," Tom said to Fella later. "I didn't know dogs could talk."

"Neither did I," said the horse. . . .

Jack: What would you say if you saw nine horses rolling over in the grass wearing red straw hats, and one horse rolling over in the grass wearing a green straw hat?

Jill: Nine out of ten horses wear red straw hats?

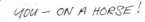

Black Beauty and the Baker's Dozen

"**G**ood morning, Beauty. Rise and shine. Time to start another day."

The cheerful voice of Mr Pickersgale the baker sounded in the yard, and Black Beauty's stable door was opened wide. It was seven o'clock on a fresh spring morning.

Beauty sniffed the air, stretched his legs as he walked into the yard, and soon started work on his morning feed of oats and fresh water. Mr Pickersgale smiled as he watched the fine horse, and then began to load the small cart with baskets of muffins, bread and crusty rolls, As usual, he had been up since five o'clock that morning, baking the day's batch of orders.

Beauty was 'on loan' to Mr Pickersgale for just two weeks, while the baker's own horse, Sugar, was recovering from a bout of influenza, and had to be kept dry and warm inside his stable. Beauty found that he enjoyed the work of pulling the light cart round the streets of London, delivering the bread to Mr Pickersgale's many customers.

As soon as Beauty was harnessed to the cart they set off. It was very quiet at first, with the only sound being the clip-clop of Beauty's hoofs as he trotted along the cobbled streets. Later on though, the city began to 'wake up'. Curtains were opened at the windows of the houses, and they passed many men and women on their way to work.

Mr Pickersgale had a cheery greeting for most of them, and they called back to him, or waved across the street as they set up various kinds of market stalls.

By this time too, some of Mr Pickersgale's customers were awake, and some of them were watching out for him on their doorsteps, if they wanted special orders that day. One lady wanted an extra half-dozen muffins for a children's tea party, and while Mr Pickersgale was fetching them from the cart she went over to pat Beauty, and to give him some tasty slices of apple.

"How's your Sugar, Mr Pickersgale?" she asked. "We haven't seen him for a day or two."

"He's down with a chill, madam," replied the baker, "but he should be up and about in a couple of weeks. Meanwhile, Beauty here is a fine replacement, as you can see."

It seemed that the morning would pass quietly on, very much as usual, but as things were to turn out, something quite out of the ordinary happened, even before Mr Pickersgale could make his next call. . . .

They were passing a large, imposing house, where usually the baker delivered a large order each day. But for a week now the family had been on holiday, visiting friends in the north of

England, so there was no delivery to be made.

Mr Pickersgale glanced at the house as they passed. But then something, just a slight movement, caught his eye. He reined Beauty in, and looked again. But now there was nothing at all to be seen, and he decided that he must have been mistaken.

He urged Beauty on – but Beauty stayed put. Mr Pickersgale hadn't been mistaken about that movement. Beauty had seen it too. His keen senses had picked up the sight of a slight movement, the sound of a footfall, and something else: the smell of smoke. Beauty knew there was something wrong.

He whinnied, and pawed the ground, and Mr Pickersgale, feeling decidedly uneasy by now, decided to investigate further. He climbed down from the cart and walked quietly to the side of the house. A side window was open, and it had obviously been forced.

Mr Pickersgale looked round for a stout stick before he climbed through the window himself, alert for attack from the intruder, whoever he might be. The window opened into the scullery, and the door to the main kitchen was ajar. The baker walked steadily forward, pushed open the door, and went into the kitchen.

The door slammed behind him with a bang. He spun round, wrenched the door open again, and was just in time to see a raggedly-dressed young boy clambering out of the window.

"Stop! Thief!" he shouted – but he knew it was no use. Even by the time he reached the window the boy was fifty yards away and running like a hare. It would be useless to give chase.

And anyway, by this time there was something else on the baker's mind. As soon as he had stepped into the kitchen he had smelled what clever Black Beauty had smelled even from outside – smoke. There was something on fire in the cellar, and if he didn't act quickly it might cause serious damage.

The trap door to the cellar was open, and looking down he could see that it was a pile of papers and rags which had caught alight. Mr Pickersgale thought quickly. There was a well at the back of the house, he knew, but it would take too much time to run backwards and forwards with several pails of water.

Then, in another corner of the cellar, he spotted a heavy, thick rug. "That's it!" he cried. He dragged it out, clambered through the window, ran to the well, winched up a pail of water, and pushed the rug right into it, soaking it completely. Now that it was wet, of course, the rug was very heavy indeed, and Mr Pickersgale was puffing and panting as he climbed through that window for the third time, flinging the rug through before him.

He was down the cellar steps in an instant, and with one great effort he took hold of one end of the soaking rug, and flung it over the fire. It doused the fire instantly, and poor Mr Pickersgale, very relieved but quite exhausted from his efforts, sat down on the cellar steps and took a well-earned rest.

As he sat there on the steps, trying to get his breath back, Mr Pickersgale heard a loud whinny. He went out into the scullery, and there was Beauty, with his head through the open window, obviously trying to find out what was going on.

"Hello there, boy," smiled Mr Pickersgale. "It's all right now, I've put the fire out. Pity I didn't catch that young hooligan, though. Didn't even get a proper look at him, in fact. I expect *you* saw him when he ran past you, but you won't be able to describe him to PC Williams, will you? Anyway, that's where we'd better be off now – to the Police Station."

Police Constable Williams listened to the story with interest, and assured the baker that he would send someone round to the house to make sure it was securely locked again, and that the fire was completely out.

"The Fosdykes won't be back for a week," he said, "but I'll wager they'll want to give you a reward. Jim Fosdyke's a rich man, and that lad might have got away with a fair amount of valuables if you hadn't disturbed him. I can't understand why he should want to start a fire though. Just a young trouble-maker, I suppose."

"Well, I'll be on my way now, PC Williams," said Mr Pickersgale. "I'm late with my deliveries and some of my customers will have gone without muffins at breakfast time."

Black Beauty and the baker completed their day's round with no further excitement, and it seemed that the whole incident had ended there. But it hadn't quite. . . .

A week later they were halfway through the usual round, and passing along a street in one of the poorer areas of London. All of a sudden, Black Beauty started acting rather strangely. He stopped, refused to move any further, pawed the ground with his foot, and turned his head sharply to the right.

For a moment Mr Pickersgale was puzzled. Whatever was the matter with Beauty? And what was he looking at, so intently? All Mr Pickersgale could see was a street urchin, tossing a ball against the wall of a house.

And then suddenly he understood. This was the boy who had broken into the Fosdykes' house. Black Beauty had recognised him, and though he couldn't speak, he was doing his best to let Mr Pickersgale know.

"All right, Beauty, I understand," he said

29

softly to the horse, and he quietly got down from the cart, walked casually over towards the boy, and then, when he was near enough, he grabbed him by the collar.

The boy gave a cry of surprise, stared at the man, and immediately recognised him. He tried to struggle free, but Mr Pickersgale was strong, and soon had him in a tight grip.

"Now then, young man," said Mr Pickersgale sternly, "you can come along with me. You've some explaining to do – to Police Constable Williams."

"Oh no, sir! Please, sir! Don't take me there, sir!" cried the boy, with a terrified look on his face. "I didn't mean no 'arm. I weren't going to steal nothing valuable. I only wanted some food from the kitchen. It's me little brother – he's ailin', and my mam can't afford to buy the good food he needs."

There was something about the boy which struck Mr Pickersgale as sincere, but he wasn't quite convinced yet. He had another question to ask. "How do you explain starting a fire which could have burnt down the whole house?"

"I didn't mean to, sir. Honest, I didn't. I only wanted to see into their cellars. We live in an attic, see, and I ain't never been in a cellar. I lit a match to see better, but I dropped it when I 'eard you comin'. I didn't 'ave time to stamp it out, but I crept back to the 'ouse later on, to make sure you'd put it out. Honest I did, sir."

Mr Pickersgale had made up his mind what to do. "All right, lad," he said. "I'll give you the benefit of the doubt. Take me to your home, and if what you say is true, we'll forget all about it."

"Oh, thank you, sir, thank you!" cried the boy. "Can I ride in the cart behind your fine 'orse?"

Jimmy started work the following Monday, and soon proved to be a nimble, quick and willing worker. Mr Pickersgale helped Jimmy's family find better accommodation than their attic rooms, and his little brother's health soon improved.

The other 'invalid' in this story, Mr Pickersgale's horse Sugar, made a great improvement too, and soon it was time for Black Beauty to go back home. The baker would have liked to have kept him, as he had grown very fond of the fine stallion, but of course Beauty had only been 'on loan'.

Before he went though, there was a final 'happy ending', when the Fosdykes returned from their stay in the North. They were so grateful to Mr Pickersgale that they invited him to a fine supper, and when they heard the truth about Jimmy's reasons for breaking in, they invited him along too.

They presented Mr Pickersgale with a reward of twelve silver crowns, and to show Jimmy that he was quite forgiven they presented him with a newly-minted golden sovereign.

Mr Pickersgale sat back after his delicious meal, looked at the thirteen shiny coins on the table, and said, "That's what I call a real baker's dozen!"

They soon reached the boy's home and, as he had said, it was just two attic rooms. The family were obviously very poor, but the boy's mother was doing her best to make their home comfortable and clean for them.

She looked very worried when she heard Mr Pickersgale's story of what had happened. "Oh Jimmy," she said to her son, "haven't I told you never to steal and never to beg? How could you?"

She turned to Mr Pickersgale. "We're having a struggle to make ends meet, sir, and that's for sure," she said. "My husband's in steady work, but it don't pay much, and I won't have little Jimmy working from morn till night in a gloomy factory. He's not a bad boy, sir. Please don't be too harsh with him."

Mr Pickersgale had been thinking hard ever since he had gone into the attic rooms, and now he had a suggestion to make. "Jimmy," he said, "do you think you would like to learn the bakery trade? My round's getting bigger, and I've been thinking of taking on a lad to help me out. You'd be on trial, mind, for a month or two, till I see how well you can work."

The joyful smiles which lit up the faces of both Jimmy and his mother were quite sufficient to give Mr Pickersgale the answer to his question.

STORYBOOK STEEDS

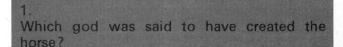

You all know, of course, that Anna Sewell wrote *Black Beauty* to draw attention to the ill-treatment of many horses in Victorian times, but horses also appear in many other stories and rhymes. Do you know:

1.
Which god was said to have created the horse?

2.
In what famous story-poem by Spenser does a horse appear whose name means 'Golden Bridle'?

3.
In which book by Harrison Ainsworth does a mare appear which was said to have been ridden by Dick Turpin?

4.
Rosinante, all skin and bone, was the horse of a man who gave his name to the book in which they both appear. Who was he?

5.
Who could all the king's horses and all the king's men not put together again?

6.
"Throughout the wide border" whose steed was the best?

7.
Who borrowed a horse from his friend the calender to ride to the Bell at Edmonton?

8.
Of what famous horse did Virgil write?

9.
In Chaucer's *Canterbury Tales* he mentions a magic brazen horse. What is the horse's name?

10.
In tales of Greek mythology what is the name of Odin's horse?

Check your answers on page 60

FOXHUNTER

Foxhunter . . . a big bay horse who captured the hearts of the public, and earned himself a place in the history of show jumping. He and his owner, Colonel Harry Llewellyn, rode to victory in many an international competition, and they helped to establish Britain as one of the world's great show jumping nations. Together they won 78 international competitions, and that doesn't include their appearances with the British team; a record that no other partnership has ever broken.

Foxhunter was everything a horse should be: big, handsome, good-tempered, intelligent and a natural jumper. He was born in Norfolk in 1940, and from an early age his love of jumping was obvious. When he was a year old he was sold to a Mr Holmes of Leicestershire, and for several seasons he hunted with Britain's finest pack of hounds, the Quorn.

However, his fine style and natural jumping ability led Mr Holmes to enter Foxhunter in show jumping competitions, and in 1946 he won several prizes. The sport was not as popular as it is today, but a Colonel Harry Llewellyn, who had just left the army, had decided to try his hand, and with this in mind he bought Foxhunter.

A great bond of friendship sprang up between the two partners, although the Colonel realised that Foxhunter had several faults in style that would have to be corrected before he could become a top class show jumper. The horse was quick to learn, and soon they were winning major competitions all over the world.

Their success made them an obvious choice for the 1948 Olympics, and as part of the British team they won a bronze medal. Four years later, at the 1952 Olympics in Helsinki, the Colonel and Foxhunter pulled off the only clear round of the Games to win a gold medal for the British team.

Nearer home there was the King George V Gold Cup at the International Horse Show. Riders all over the world spend a lifetime trying to win this most coveted of trophies. Foxhunter and Colonel Harry Llewellyn won it three times, a record that remains unbroken.

By now public interest in the sport, and particularly in Foxhunter, was tremendous. Young fans put pictures of the famous pair on their walls, and the Colonel received hundreds of letters and presents. Carrots, bags of sugar, and many other horsey delicacies arrived regularly for Foxhunter.

Finally, in 1956, after ten successful years, the Colonel and Foxhunter retired from the show jumping scene. They were not forgotten, and when Foxhunter died in 1959 he was mourned by thousands. He and the Colonel had become a legend in their own time, and their equal has yet to be found.

A CLEAR ROUND?

Here's a horse-jumping game to play with your friends. It's simple, and lots of fun, and all you need to play are a selection of counters (one for each person) a dice and a pencil and paper.

Place all the counters on the starting line and, in turn, throw the dice, moving your counter the appropriate number of squares along the course. If you land on an obstacle square (the ones with horseshoes around them) you must read the penalty, and jot down your penalty score as you go along. The first person to complete the course has no time faults, but the second to finish has five penalty faults added to his score; the third has ten penalty points; the fourth fifteen penalty points, and so on. The winner is the player with the *least* number of faults.

Raise a horse laugh!

A camel is a warped horse.

Cowboy: "Did the horse I lent you behave itself?"
City Dude: "Sure, when it came to a fence, it let me go over first!"

When is a boy like a pony?
When he's a little hoarse.

A farmer was driving his horse and cart along the road with his old dog Rover sitting beside him in the cart. Suddenly the horse turned round and said, "Gee, isn't it hot?"

The farmer was amazed. "Fancy my horse talking!" he cried.

"Oh, yes, but he's just like everyone else," replied Rover. "All he can ever talk about is the weather!"

Why did the man get behind the donkey?
Because he thought he'd get a kick out of it

HORSEPOWER!

The hedgerows that stretched straight and low by the side of the canal were alive with the sounds of birds and insects, and the towpath stretched its lazy way towards the dimming sun on the horizon. The only sounds that could be heard were the dim ripples of the flat, still water.

Black Beauty was happy with his new owners. He had been apprehensive when he realised that he had been sold to canal people, but he enjoyed his quiet life by the water. He found that pulling the barge along the straight ribbons of criss-crossing canals was an easy, pleasant life, and he was well treated.

But Black Beauty's happiness was not shared by his owner. Sam Seaton was a worried man, for he feared that he might lose his barge, the *Jinty*. Sam hadn't worked the canals all his life; in fact, he'd had the *Jinty* for only five months, and still owed money for her. If business didn't improve soon, Sam would have to give up the barge to Smeech, her previous owner.

Sam had turned to a life on the canals when his wife had died. They had worked as cook and gardener at a large country estate, and when his wife had died, Sam had been turned out of his small tied cottage. With what savings he had,

Sam had put a deposit on the *Jinty*, hoping to make a home and a living for himself and his young daughter, Molly.

But times were hard for all the canal people, and the Seatons' latest cargo, a ton of coal to be taken to Setborough, would hardly earn enough to pay for Beauty's fodder. All these thoughts flooded through Sam's mind as the *Jinty* made her slow, steady way through the countryside.

The only cheerful member of the Seaton family was Molly – just ten years old, and very happy in her new home on the barge. She didn't go to school very often, but Molly didn't mind that at all – she was happiest in the open air, with the freedom to do as she pleased. Molly whistled happily as she led Black Beauty along the tow-path. "I know Pa's worried about paying Smeech the money we owe him," she said quietly. "But I'm sure something will turn up for us. I hope it does, anyway, for I don't think Pa could bear to lose the *Jinty*."

The coal was unloaded at Setborough, the *Jinty*'s home base, and Black Beauty was rewarded with a bag of oats. Now was the time to wait – to wait to see if anyone offered them another job; to wait to see if Smeech came asking for his money.

The job didn't materialise, but Smeech did. He was a mean-looking, hand-wringing man, and he smiled a thin smile as he approached. "Well, Seaton," he called. "You got any money for me this time? Two crowns you still owe on this barge, and you know what'll happen if I don't get my money, don't you? The barge will be mine again!"

Smeech looked happy at the thought of turning the Seatons off and selling the barge again. "Well, have you got it?"

Sam Seaton looked distastefully at Smeech, and wished he'd never set eyes on the man. "No, I haven't got your two crowns for you," he said. "You know times are bad on the canals, and there isn't much work around. Just give me a bit longer, Smeech, and you'll get your money. I give you my word."

"Hard cash is what I want," said Smeech. "Not your word. I'll give you just two weeks from today to come up with the money. If I don't have the two crowns by then, I'll have you off! Hear me?"

"Yes, I hear you all right," said Sam Seaton sadly, as he watched Smeech stride off into the town. "Well, Molly," he said. "I think we can say goodbye to the barge. There's not much hope of us earning the money in two weeks. Look," he said, pointing to all the other barges that lay idle by the canal side, "there's no work for anyone."

For two days the *Jinty* lay moored to the canal side, then on the third day a stranger came walking along the towpath. He looked a prosperous man, and Sam watched, downcast, as he stopped at the first barge and talked to the owner. He was probably offering the Browns a good job. . . .

But the man soon left the Brown barge and stopped at the next. Here again he spoke to the owner for a few moments, then strode on. Soon he approached the *Jinty*, and held out his hand to Sam. "Good day to you," he said. "My name is James Bollington, and I have a cargo of fine linen for Matcham. Do you want the job?"

Sam couldn't believe his luck. "Why, yes, sir, of course," he said. "Be glad to!" But then he paused. "But why did the other bargees refuse the cargo? Is there some catch?"

"Not a catch," said Bollington. "I was just going to explain. The reason the others refused is that I want this cargo delivered to Matcham within the week. The others said it couldn't be done."

"A week!" said Sam. "They're right, it can't be done. Matcham's a good ten days' journey from here."

"Yes, I know that," said Bollington. "And that's why I'm prepared to pay five crowns to the man who'll get my cargo there for me!"

Molly Seaton had been listening to the conversation, and couldn't keep quiet for a minute longer. "Take the job, Pa," she said. "We can do it, I know we can!"

Sam looked at Molly, then at Black Beauty. "It'll be hard work for all three of us," he said. "But it's the only way to save the *Jinty*. Yes, Mr Bollington, we'll get your linen to Matcham for you!"

So the bargain was struck, and the bales of fine linen were loaded in the Jinty's spacious holds. It was already late afternoon, but Sam Seaton knew that he had no time to spare. "No time for idling now, girl," he said to Molly. "Harness Beauty and we'll be off."

So the *Jinty* began her long journey along the flat, smooth waters of the canal.

For days the Seatons kept up to the schedule Sam had set for them, travelling for fourteen hours every day, and stopping only to sleep and to feed and rest Black Beauty. Sam realised that Beauty was a fine horse, for he seemed to sense what he had to do and was always willing to travel further. Sam almost began to think that they were going to make it to Matcham on time.

On the fourth day Molly peered into the distance along the towpath. "Hebley Bridge coming up," she said. "Hope we get through all right, Pa."

Hebley Bridge was a long, low bridge that spanned the canal. There was no towpath for Beauty to walk along, so Molly took him up past the bridge, and gave him a well-earned rest as they waited for the *Jinty* to emerge from the other side. Now it was Sam Seaton's turn to power the barge through the tunnel. . . .

The only way for Sam to get the barge through was to use his feet. He had to lie on his back on the cabin roof and 'walk' his feet along the roof of the tunnel. It was slow going, and very hard work, and Sam was relieved when he saw a chink of daylight at the far end of the tunnel. As he emerged, Molly ran towards him.

"Well done, Pa," she said. "If you can get us through Hebley Bridge so easily, the rest of the trip'll be plain sailing!"

Tom looked apologetic. "You'll not make Matcham this night," he said, waving his hand towards the lock. "The lock mechanism's failed, and the engineers won't be here to repair it until tomorrow. Sorry, Sam, but there's no way through."

Sam rubbed his thick fingers through his unruly hair. "Oh, no," he said. "What am I going to do now? If I don't earn the money from this cargo, we'll lose the *Jinty*. . . ."

"I'm sorry, Sam, but there's nothing I can do," said Tom. "Now, will you come to the inn for that ale? You look as though you could do with a bit of cheering up."

Sam Seaton followed Tom down the towpath to the inn, leaving Molly and Beauty standing by the old barge. Molly ran her fingers along the cracked and faded paintwork and turned to Black Beauty. "I can't bear to think of losing the *Jinty*," she said. "I must think of something."

Suddenly Molly smiled. "There *is* a way of getting Mr Bollington's linen to Matcham on time," she said. "This is what we'll do: the only way to get the bales there is to carry them one by one! I'll load them onto your back, Beauty, and we'll ride into Matcham with them! It's only a mile beyond the lock – I'm sure we can do it!"

Molly leapt down into the hold and emerged with a large bale of linen, which she strapped onto Beauty's broad back. Beauty seemed to understand what he had to do, and he galloped off at a good pace, straight down the towpath into Matcham.

The warehouseman stared in amazement as Beauty stopped, and Molly heaved down the huge bale of linen. "That's the first part of Mr

The night before they were due in Matcham, Sam and Molly sat in their cabin, drinking mugs of warm cocoa. "We've got until eight o'clock tomorrow night," said Sam. "I think we're going to make it!"

But Sam and Molly had no idea what was going to happen the next day. The last lock they had to pass before sailing into Matcham was the one at Jack's Dike. Sam looked forward to passing, for Tom, the lock-keeper, was a good friend of his.

As they drew near to the lock, Sam leapt from the *Jinty* and shook hands with Tom.

"Good to see you again," said Tom. "Will you take a mug of ale with me in the inn?"

"I'd like to," said Sam, "but I can't. I've a very special cargo to get to Matcham before eight this evening. I know I've time to spare, but I don't want to take any chances. I must get on."

Bollington's cargo of linen," she gasped. "I'll be back with the rest later!" Without another word, Molly leapt onto Beauty's back and they galloped off back to the barge.

It was hot work in the afternoon sun, and Molly and Beauty were soon tired, but even Beauty seemed to understand how important it was to get the cargo to Matcham, and he galloped as fast as he could, back and forth to Matcham.

When Sam Seaton emerged from the inn he was amazed to see Molly and Black Beauty riding from the direction of Matcham. "What are you two up to?" he asked.

"We've been to Matcham," said Molly, leaping down. "We've already delivered three bales of linen. Black Beauty has taken over from the *Jinty*!"

Sam Seaton smiled sadly. "Thanks for trying to help, gal, but you'll never do it," he said. "I know Black Beauty's a strong, willing horse, but he'll never do it. He's tired now."

Molly was angry. "Well, I think we *will* do it," she said. "I want to save the *Jinty* if I can. *I'm* not giving up, and neither is Black Beauty!"

Molly's words had a sobering effect on Sam. "You're right, you know," he said, jumping to his feet. "We *can* do it!"

And while Molly loaded another bale onto Beauty's back, Sam found what he was looking for in the hedgerow. He bound two stout branches together to make a sort of litter, then loaded a bale onto it, tying it securely with twine. 'I must be mad,' he thought to himself as he set off at a jog towards Matcham, 'but if Molly and Black Beauty are giving it a try, I'll try too!'

You can imagine the surprised warehouseman when the next consignment of Mr Bollington's linen arrived at Matcham, pulled along on a litter by Sam Seaton. "Well I never," said the amazed man, lifting his cap to scratch his head. "I've never seen anything like it in all my born days. . . ."

Sam Seaton laughed. "See you in about an hour," he said, and set off back down the towpath.

So the routine continued, but soon all three

were tired and weary. It was only the thought of Smeech owning the *Jinty* that put new energy into Sam's legs. . . .

As dusk fell over the canal a small group of people gathered outside the warehouse, for word had spread of the strange goings on, and everyone wanted to see if the Seatons would make the deadline. As Sam staggered into the warehouse at seven o'clock with yet another heavy bale he staggered, then dropped to the floor. Black Beauty had just arrived too, and Sam turned to his daughter. "I can't move another step," he said. "But there's just one more bale on the *Jinty*. It's up to you and Black Beauty now."

That was all Molly needed to hear, and after giving Black Beauty a few more moments rest, they set off again, soon disappearing into the darkness that had fallen over the canal bank.

The throng of people at the warehouse was joined by Mr Bollington. "Well, Seaton, I hear you've had some troubles," he said. "Have you managed to get my cargo here on time?"

"All but one bale," said Sam. "But you'll have your cargo here by eight, as I promised." And Sam crossed his fingers and peered into the gloom, straining his ears for the sound of hooves on the cobbled path.

It was just before eight o'clock when someone from the back of the crowd shouted out. "Hooves!" the voice cried. "I can hear hooves!"

Sure enough, the crowd soon heard the steady *clip*, *clop* of hooves, and as Molly and Black Beauty came into sight there was a great cheer, and the last bale of linen was lifted from Black Beauty's tired back.

"Well done!" said Sam Seaton, patting Beauty's back gratefully.

"Yes, well done, all three of you!" said Mr Bollington, handing over five shining new crowns. "You've certainly earned your pay today!"

"Yes, we have that," said Sam, putting an arm around his daughter, and rubbing Beauty's nose. "Thanks to a bit of horsepower, we've saved the *Jinty*!"

BUFFALO BILL'S HORSES

Behind every great man there's . . . no, not a woman in Buffalo Bill's case, but a string of remarkable horses.

William F Cody, better known to us as Buffalo Bill, became a legendary name in the Wild West of America, gaining fame as a hunter, scout, sure-fire shot and entertainer. But all the things he did so well depended on one thing above all others — his close relationship with his horses, which were indispensable in the life he led.

He began his horse riding very early, and was such a good rider that when he was just fifteen years old he joined the famous band of Pony Express riders who carried the mail from one side of America to the other. He did, in fact, set the record for the longest ride in the history of the Express: a staggering 384 miles, on one horse!

Soon after, Bill started to earn his living as a hunter, riding an Indian pony called Brigham. Brigham wasn't a handsome horse, but he was swift and sure, and the two formed a perfect partnership. Bill was working for the Kansas Pacific Railway, hunting buffalo to feed the workers who were building the line, and he was such a successful hunter that he earned his nickname of Buffalo Bill. Brigham proved himself to be a strong fearless horse. The huge buffalo would swerve danger-

ously, but Brigham wasn't worried; he would gallop alongside them, giving Bill just enough time to squeeze off two shots. If Bill didn't hit the target, Brigham would gallop away from the herd before approaching again, until his master hit the target.

Bill's second Indian horse was a large yellow horse called Buckskin Joe. Joe was a very large horse by Indian standards, and as soon as Bill set eyes on him he knew he just had to own him, so he bought him from the Pawnee scout who owned him. Bill was by this time also working as a Scout for the US cavalry, and Buckskin Joe was perfectly suited to this job, eating up the miles with his long legs.

When he rode on ahead of the troops to scout the land, Bill used to ride one horse, and lead Buckskin Joe behind. If there was a hint of danger ahead — which there usually was! — Bill would leap onto Buckskin Joe's back, and the horse would

carry him swiftly to safety.

One day Buffalo Bill and his horses came across a group of over a hundred hostile Indian braves, and Bill knew that his only chance of safety lay in the nearest fort, 195 miles away! Leaping onto Joe's back, Bill made for the fort. One by one the Indian horses tired and stopped, but still Buckskin Joe ran on, and carried Bill safely to the fort. But Joe paid the price for his gallant effort, for he was so exhausted and weak after the run that he went blind. Bill knew that he would have to get another horse, but he couldn't bear to sell Buckskin Joe, so he retired him to one of his ranches, where he lived out his life in ease and comfort. When he died he was buried under a tombstone that read:

Old Buckskin Joe, the horse that on several occasions saved the life of Buffalo Bill, by carrying him safely out of the range of Indian bullets.

Some years later, Buffalo Bill gave up scouting, and formed his famous Wild West Show, a thrilling spectacle that featured fancy shooting, bronco busting, Indian war dances, and a mock Indian raid on a stage coach. One of the star attractions, along with Bill, Annie Oakley and Sitting Bull, was Charlie, Bill's most famous horse.

Bill bought Charlie when he was five years old, a half-breed Kentucky horse, part Thorough-bred, and it was as Bill broke him in that he realised he had found a horse of remarkable strength and intelligence. Horse and rider became inseparable, and Bill taught and coached what he thought of as the per-fect horse.

Charlie was a real star attrac-tion in Buffalo Bill's Wild West Show. He performed perfectly as Bill acted out a sharp-shoot-ing display, shattering glass balls that were thrown high into the air over the arena. And he took part in the mock attack on a stagecoach, making his way, riderless, through the shouting and confusion, always by Bill's side.

In 1887, when Charlie (now known as Old Charlie) was twenty years old, the whole Wild West Show was trans-ported to England, where they took part in a very popular tour. Charlie was a great favourite with the crowds, and earned the admiration of the Prince of Wales, who watched a special Royal Performance of the show at Windsor Castle.

The next year, after a triumph-ant tour, the show left England, and it was on the voyage home that Old Charlie caught a chill and died. Buffalo Bill had many other horses after that, but none was as dear to him as Old Charlie.

HORSE RIDDLES

What is it that has four legs, eats oats, has a tail and sees equally well from both ends?

A blind horse.

If you took a ride on a donkey, what fruit would you resemble?

A pear (pair).

What is the principal part of a horse?

His mane part.

What creature always goes to bed with his shoes on?

A horse.

Why is a girl on a horse like a cloud?

Because they both hold the reins.

How can you make a slow horse fast?

Don't give him anything to eat.

Horses of the Bible

Horses and donkeys feature in several important events in the Bible.

Old Testament

In the Old Testament Noah took donkeys, asses and horses into the Ark with him during the Flood, and it was in a chariot of fire drawn by horses that the prophet Elijah was taken up to Heaven at the end of his life.

When Joseph became powerful in the land of Egypt and was once more reunited with the brothers who had sold him into slavery many years before, he forgave them and he sent as a gift to his aged father Jacob twenty asses laden with corn, bread and meat.

A wise man named Balaam had an ass which saved him from death. The ass saw an angel which barred their way to the city of Moab where the king wanted the death of the children of Israel. The angel finally allowed Balaam to see him too, and he told Balaam how to appease King Balak's anger.

New Testament

It was in a stable, in a manger, among the horses and donkeys, that the Baby Jesus was born, and when Mary and Joseph had to flee with the baby into Egypt to escape Herod's wrath, it was a humble ass that carried the Holy Family to safety.

Later, in one of the best known of all the parables, Jesus told of how a Samaritan befriended a man who fell among thieves, binding up his wounds, and placing him on his own donkey to take him to the safety and comfort of an inn.

And just before the pain of Calvary, Jesus rode one day into Jerusalem seated upon an ass, while his followers strewed palm leaves in front of him . . . thus starting the custom of Palm Sunday which is followed in Christian churches today.

Horse superstitions and snippets

Bit of my own back again

In order to seal a bargain and to ensure that all went well with the purchase, horse dealers would always give the buyer a few of his own coins back again. This custom was more prevalent in the north of England and, strangely enough, if the buyer did not get 'a bit of my own back again' the horses often suffered several complaints!

Bad Luck For Jockeys

Jockeys are a very superstitious group and no jockey will willingly have his photograph taken on his mount before a race because he thinks that it will bring him bad luck. A jockey also thinks that if he loses his whip before the race this means he could also lose the race, and another bad luck bringer is if a jockey's boots are placed on the floor of the dressing room before a race!

Lucky Horseshoes

Horseshoes have always been symbols of good luck, being given both in their original iron forms or as ceremonial symbols of good luck to the bride and groom on their wedding day. Many door knockers take the form of a good luck horseshoe, and Lord Nelson had a horseshoe nailed to the mast of HMS Victory. A horseshoe also hangs over the door of several country churches, and a form of good wishes in olden times was: 'May the horseshoe never be pulled from your threshold.'

Stockings and Horses

It is lucky to own a horse with both forelegs wearing white 'socks', but if one foreleg and one hind leg wear stockings bad luck will follow. However, another superstition contradicts this, saying that fore and hind stockings are lucky, while a horse with only one white stocking brings ill-fortune!

Horse WORDS

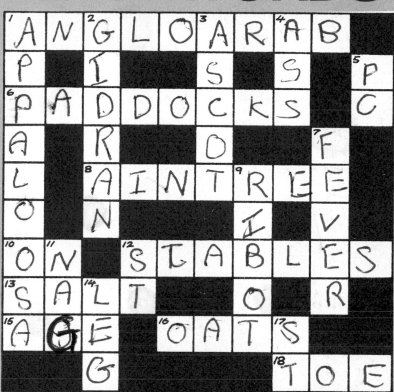

1 A	N	2 G	L	O	3 A	R	4 A	B	■
P	■	I	■	■	S	■	S	■	5 P
6 P	A	D	D	O	C	K	S	■	C
A	■	R	■	■	O	■	■	7 F	■
L	■	8 A	I	N	T	9 R	E	E	■
O	■	N	■	■	■	I	■	V	■
10 O	11 N	■	12 S	T	A	B	L	E	S
13 S	A	14 L	T	■	■	O	■	R	■
15 A	G	E	■	16 O	A	T	17 S	■	■
■	■	G	■	■	■	■	18 T	O	E

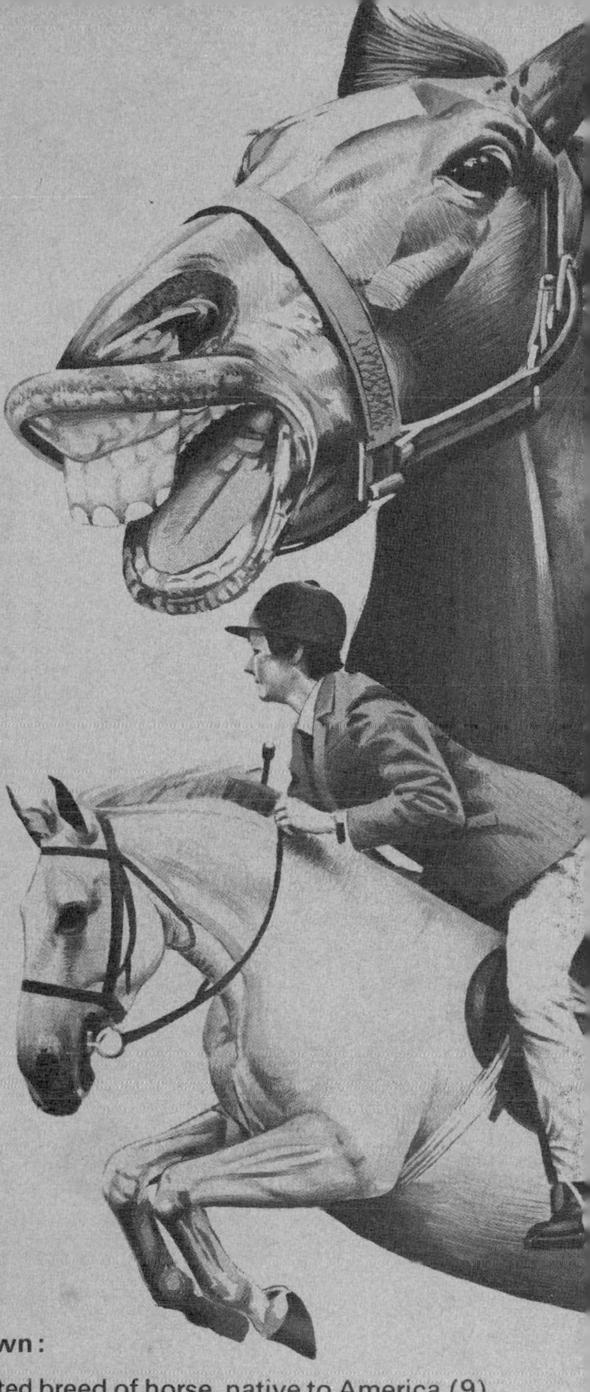

Clues Across:

1. Sounding like a West/East alliance, this breed is the ideal saddle-horse (5-4)
6. Where horses spend their time when not in the stables (8)
8. Racecourse where the Grand National is run (7)
10. Riding . . horseback (2)
12. Horse homes (7)
13. A . . . .-lick is something horses appreciate in hot weather (4)
15. You can tell this by looking in a horse's mouth (3)
16. A popular horse food (4)
18. The hoof is really the horse's one remaining one (3)

Clues Down:

1. A spotted breed of horse, native to America (9)
2. A breed of Hungarian heavy horse (6)
3. Famous British racecourse (5)
4. A silly horse? (3)
5. A meeting place for young horses? (initials) (2)
7. A horse ailment, characterised by a very high temperature (5)
9. A great racehorse, foaled in the 1950s (5)
11. A worrying horse? (3)
12. The . . Leger is a famous race (2)
14. The pedal and cannon bones are both found here (3)
17. . . Paddy was a famous winner of 12 down (2)

Turn to page 60 to check your answers

salvation for black beauty!

As he bent his head to eat the lovely bran mash young Joe Sharpe had put before him, Black Beauty whinnied contentedly. Life with the Sharpe family, who sold fruit and vegetables in a little corner shop in the east end of London, was hard but happy.

Each morning Beauty and Matt Sharpe, together with Joe, went off to market early to buy the best produce for the shop. Matt had a good eye for what was good and cheap, and they usually came back with a cart full of fresh produce which was easy to sell in the shop. It was not often that much remained at the end of the day; anything that was left, Mrs Sharpe readily made into a tasty supper dish.

Suddenly Beauty became aware that Joe and Matt were talking about him.

"Pa, after the shop closes tomorrow, can I borrow Beauty and the cart?" asked Joe anxiously. "Mr Booth's son William has asked me to go down to the market with him and ask the farmers and stallholders if we can have any potatoes or carrots or a few apples that are left. William says his mother is opening a soup kitchen down at the mission they run in Whitechapel, and she needs vegetables to stock up the pot."

"I bet she does," growled Matt, rather gruffly. "Still, clergyman Booth and his family are doing a fine job trying to help the poor, and keeping the drunkards out of the taverns. If they don't spend all their money on drink, perhaps some of them will spend a bit in our shop. But I don't know as how I holds with this new army which folks say he has started. A clergyman as a General in an army . . . whatever next, is what I say!"

"But, Pa, it's a Christian army, its soldiers are only battling for the salvation of souls!" explained Joe eagerly. "Let me go, please, Pa. I promise you that I won't get into any trouble."

"Well, see that you don't then, boy, and make sure Beauty comes to no harm, either," said Matt Sharpe. "He's too valuable a horse to lose . . . even for the sake of someone's salvation!"

Joe thought this a rather uncharitable remark of his father's, but he wisely said nothing, only too pleased to have had his request granted so quickly.

However, beneath Matt's brusque exterior was a kind heart, and when Joe and his friend Will set off with Beauty they found a sack of potatoes and a bunch of carrots as his father's contribution to the soup kitchen.

At the market the boys fared quite well, for many of the men had relatives who were in the new Salvation Army, and they liked the gentle Mrs Booth who showed her sympathy in such a practical way.

Soon the cart was filled with vegetables, even if some of them were slightly rotten.

"Have no fear, my mother will soon cut out the rotten part," said Will. "We have done well, thanks to you and Beauty, Joe."

"Well, it is no thanks to me!" sneered one man who had overheard the conversation. "If the poor can't feed themselves, let them starve!"

Joe flushed with anger at these words and would have answered back hotly, but Will pulled on Beauty's reins and set off quickly to the mission.

"Don't tangle with Jack Johnson if you can help it, Joe," he said. "He's a real troublemaker. He jeers at all our street meetings and he is very rude to some of our Salvation lassies."

"He's a coward and a bully!" cried Joe. "And a mean man!"

"There are many like him, Joe, in this world," said Mrs Booth, coming out of the mission and overhearing Joe's words. "My, what a wonderful supply of vegetables you have there. There will be many full stomachs tonight, thanks to you . . . and Beauty, of course. He has done a fine job pulling this heavy cart. I think we might spare him just half a carrot."

Beauty accepted the carrot gratefully. He liked this woman with the care-worn hands and gentle

voice, and he noticed how the crowd of people, ragged women and children gathered around her, looked at her in wonder and gratitude.

Suddenly, Beauty pricked up his ears as the sound of music reached him.

"Here come our soldiers back from a street meeting!" cried William. "Look how proudly they walk, and why, there's Tim Tover, who only last night was thrown out of the tavern for drunkenness, marching proudly with the rest. Hallelujah, another soul saved!"

Joe watched as the procession approached, noticing several pretty girls shaking their tambourines in time to the music, while one girl went round with a small box, asking for contributions from the few well-to-do spectators in the crowd who had come down to the east end to see how the other half of London town lived.

Beauty's hoofs tapped to the gay music and Joe laughed to see him.

Then, suddenly, out of the crowd came an ugly menacing figure. He looked familiar to Joe and when he saw him open a bag of ripe, rotten tomatoes, Joe realised who it was . . . it was Jack Johnson, the mealy-mouthed uncharitable man from the vegetable market . . . and he looked as if he was all out to start trouble.

"You're singing a fine song, my beauties, let's see if these will help you to sing sweeter!" he jeered.

And before Joe's horrified eyes, Johnson began pelting the Salvation Army lassies with the rotten tomatoes.

They splattered on the girls' uniforms and one or two people in the crowd yelled encouragement to Johnson. "Aye, teach 'em a lesson, Jack, asking 'onest folk for money better spent on beer after a day's work!" shouted one of Johnson's cronies.

The girls carried on singing bravely, while Joe watched, helpless with anger.

But Beauty had already realised that something was wrong. He remembered the rough voice from the market place, and he sensed Joe's anger at the man. He reared up on his hind legs, startling the bully, who staggered and fell and he would have been run over by the cart if Joe and William had not quickly pulled him clear.

Johnson dropped his bag of rotten tomatoes and backed away from Beauty's menacing hoofs.

"Keep that animal away from me!" he shouted. "I'll have the law on you!"

"The less *you* mention the law the better!" retorted Joe, scooping up the squashed bag. "Fancy throwing tomatoes at innocent lassies! Shame on you, Jack Johnson!"

Suddenly a mischievous look came into his eyes and he added, "But it's a shame to waste what's left!" and he began to throw the remains of the tomatoes at the luckless Johnson. "How do you like being pelted with tomatoes?" he cried.

The crowd roared with laughter and Black Beauty whinnied his approval as, one after another, the rotten fruit found its target.

But the girl collecting from the crowd gently admonished Joe for his act and began to wipe the stains from Jack Johnson's coat with a dainty handkerchief.

The bully looked at her in astonishment. "If you can do this for me after what I have just done to you then there must be something in this salvation lark after all," he said, looking very ashamed of himself. "I'm sorry for all the trouble I have caused." He thrust a gold coin into the girl's hand.

Then, turning to Joe and Will, who were looking on in delight and wonder, he added, "Anytime you come collecting for the soup kitchen you can have the pick of the stall, and I'll give Beauty the best carrot I can find."

"Thanks, Jack," grinned Joe, and as he led Beauty back home he added softly into the horse's ear, "Well, old boy, we've had quite a good night's work between us. I've collected plenty of vegetables for the free soup kitchen, and you managed to squeeze a guinea out of mean old Johnson . . . and possibly make him see the error of his ways."

Black Beauty nuzzled Joe's hand gently, happy to have pleased the boy, and as Joe stroked him affectionately in return, the youth added with a laugh, "I bet you are the first four-footed soldier in General Bramwell Booth's Salvation Army!"

The Spotted Horses

Spotted horses are not in fact a breed, but are classified simply by their colouring. No one knows exactly where they originated, but they are known to have existed in ancient times, and can be seen in early Chinese art. Later they spread to Europe, and from there to America with the Spaniards.

THE APPALOOSA is descended from those Spanish horses, and until this century it was bred almost exclusively by the Nez Perce Indians of North America. They liked the spotted coat because it provided excellent natural camouflage, and they used the horses both for hunting buffalo and for fighting. As the white settlers drove the Indians from their land the horses became almost extinct, but now the Americans have formed a club to re-establish the Indian breed.

THE KNABSTUP is the Danish version of the spotted horse, and like the Appaloosa it does not conform to a distinct physical type. The coat of the spotted horse is silky smooth, and an unusual feature of the spots is that they are raised up, and can be felt with the fingers. The coat itself is usually white or pale grey, being darker at the head and neck, and the spots are either black, brown, or chestnut. Various names are given to the pattern of spots: blanket, leopard, raindrop and speckled are just some.

WHAT DO YOU KNOW?

Here's a quiz to find out how much you know about horses. To help you, all the answers begin with the letter B.

1.
One of the three Arabian sires who are the ancestors of the Thoroughbred racehorse was imported to England in 1689. What was the horse's name?

2.
What is the more common name for the cow pony of America?

3.
What was the name of Mary Queen of Scots' palfrey, which she named after the Countess of Dunbar?

4.
What is the term used to describe horses of any shade of brown from light tan to dark brown, with a black mane and tail?

5.
What is the name of a well-known breed of heavy draught horse, native to Belgium?

6.
What was Alexander the Great's famous horse called?

7.
What was the name of the mare that Dick Turpin rode on his long ride from London to York?

8.
Can you name the breed of horse, having many of the characteristics of the Arab, which is native to Algeria and Morocco?

9.
What was the Vicar of Wakefield's horse called?

10.
Rodrigo Diaz, better known as El Cid, owned a famous battle charger. What was its name?

Check your answers on page 60

A HORSE IN A MILLION

Black Beauty was working as a dray horse, delivering ale to the inns and taverns of a large north country town. He had become a great favourite with all his drivers, and with one of the inn keepers in particular, Jack Atkins of the Rose and Crown on High Street.

Jack Atkins had a little daughter called Alice, who was about ten years old, and just at that time Jack and Mrs Atkins were very worried about her. She was only just recovering from a serious illness, which had left her weak and very pale. Poor Alice lay in bed each day, taking no interest in anything which was going on around her. Her mother and father had tried everything they could think of to speed her recovery, but the most they had achieved was persuading her to spend an hour or so each day sitting in a comfortable chair by her window, looking out into the street below.

One day in early Spring, Beauty's driver was chatting with Jack, while he delivered the day's order. "How's your little Alice today?" asked the driver, and Jack sighed.

"I don't know, I'm sure," said Jack. "Doctor McPherson says she's as physically fit as she'll ever be, but the illness has left her so tired and weak, she just doesn't seem to enjoy anything any more. He says that if we can just get her interested in something, anything at all, then she'll be on the mend quick as a flash. But we're at our wits' end, the pair of us."

"Have you tried getting her some new toys?"

"There's a roomful up there!" replied Jack, nodding towards the window of little Alice's room. "She just looks at 'em, picks 'em up, and then quietly puts 'em aside. We've had all her little friends in to see her, but she doesn't join in their chatter, and sooner or later they get bored and go

back out to play. You can't blame them, they're only youngsters, and they don't understand what's the matter with her. Come to the point, neither do Mary and me!"

"Maybe when the summer weather comes she'll perk up," said the driver, trying to cheer Jack up. "Let's hope she'll be better for the brewery's annual picnic to Cherry Tree Woods. That's only a month away, you know."

"Oh yes," said Jack Atkins, his face lighting up. "I'd forgotten about that. Yes, that might just do the trick. But we can't stand here talking all day. Let's get the barrels into the cellar – it'll be time to open in an hour. Can't have my customers going thirsty!"

Meanwhile, up in Alice's bedroom, her mother was getting the child up to spend a while by the window. Mrs Atkins spoke brightly as she helped her up, and made sure that she was warm and comfortable in the armchair. But Alice hardly answered her, and only smiled in a vague, abstracted way, as if she just couldn't be bothered with any interruptions.

Mrs Atkins looked out into the street, and saw Beauty standing below, waiting patiently until it was time to pull the dray to the next tavern. "Oh look, Alice," she said cheerfully. "Look at the fine black horse down there."

Whether it was by coincidence, or some special sixth sense, Mrs Atkins would never know. But just at that moment, Black Beauty lifted his head, looked towards the window, and gave a soft whinny.

"He's saying hello, Alice!" said Mrs Atkins delightedly, and she watched her daughter's face closely.

As she told her husband later, she couldn't really be sure whether she had imagined it or not, but she had the definite impression that an expression of brief happiness passed over the child's face. It only lasted for a second, before Alice lapsed back into her sad mood, but for Mrs Atkins it was enough to give her new hope of her daughter's eventual complete recovery.

"The horse, eh?" said her husband thoughtfully. "Well, Mary, we've a big cellar. And there's no reason why we shouldn't lay in a few extra stocks. I'll order so much beer that horse will have to come here every single day!"

And that's just what happened. At first Beauty's driver, Charlie Dixon, thought that Jack must be expanding his business, but after a few days curiosity prompted him to ask why the landlord suddenly needed so much beer. When he heard the reply he said immediately, "Well, why didn't you say so! I can bring Beauty round any day, you don't have to keep taking all this beer. Is Alice really taking an interest in him?"

"Thanks, Charlie, I'm very grateful to you," said Jack. "Mary and I have been feeling so much better these last few days. Alice really does seem to look forward to seeing the horse. She hasn't actually said anything about him yet, and we don't want to press her, for fear of pushing her too fast, but each day when Mary goes in she's always ready and waiting to sit in her chair by the window, as if she knows Beauty'll be along soon."

"That's grand news, Jack," said Charlie Dixon with a smile. "Now, how about this – I can bring Beauty twice a day, after I finish my morning and afternoon rounds. Will that be all right?"

"That will be wonderful, Charlie," said Jack Atkins. "I can't tell you how grateful I am to you."

Over the following week, Charlie kept his promise and appeared regularly outside the Rose and Crown. There was no overnight change in Alice's condition, but all three of them watched her eagerly, noting little smiles, and the odd happy phrase. "Is Black Beauty here yet?" she would ask her mother. Or, "Maybe I could ride him one day."

Beauty seemed to sense the importance of his visits, and at a word from Charlie he would lift his head and look towards the window where the little girl's pale face peeped out.

The days were getting warmer by now, and at last Alice's mother decided that it was warm

enough for her daughter to venture outside for a short while. She suggested this rather hesitantly to Alice, fearing that it might still be too much for her. But to her delight Alice replied: "All right, mother. But can I go out when Black Beauty comes to see us?"

"Of course you can," smiled Mrs Atkins, keeping her fingers crossed that all would go well.

All did go well of course – very well indeed.

There was a marked improvement in young Alice from the moment she stepped outside the door. The light Spring breeze brought some colour to her cheeks, and she smiled happily. And then, when she saw Beauty's dray turning into the yard of the Rose and Crown, she did something for which neither of her parents had really dared to hope. She let go of her mother's hand, and ran towards him.

Charlie Dixon held his breath as he watched her. He knew that one false move from Beauty now might be enough to send the child running back to her mother. But he needn't have worried. Beauty was very gentle as he lowered his head and softly nuzzled little Alice's shoulder. She cautiously put out her hand to stroke his nose, and from that moment it was obvious to each of the three people watching that a friendship had sprung up between the big stallion and little Alice, which would do more to help her recovery than all the medicine in the world.

As the weeks passed the friendship deepened, and by the time the date of the brewery's annual picnic came round little Alice was quite herself again. Charlie had offered to drive her and three of her friends in his dray, pulled by Black Beauty, of course.

Mr and Mrs Atkins climbed aboard too, and there were happy smiles all round as they clip-clopped out of the yard. Alice and her little friends chattered excitedly all along the journey to Cherry Tree Woods. The picnic was just beginning as they arrived, and several of the brewery's drays were pulling into a clearing in the woods, each loaded up with four, five, or even six children.

There was an appetising spread laid out on trestle tables, ready to be served after the usual games and the nature ramble through the woods to Cherry Tree River.

Alice and her friends scrambled down from the dray, thanked Charlie Dixon for bringing them, and said goodbye for the present to Beauty. He was going to wait with the other horses, in the cool shade beneath the trees, where they could graze at their leisure.

ANSWERS

STORYBOOK STEEDS

1. Neptune; 2. Faerie Queen; 3. Rookwood; 4. Don Quixote; 5. Humpty Dumpty; 6. Lochinvar's horse; 7. John Gilpin; 8. The Wooden Horse of Troy; 9. Cambuscan; 10. Sleipnir.

WHAT DO YOU KNOW?

1. Byerley Turk; 2. bronco; 3. Black Agnes; 4. bay; 5. Brabançon; 6. Bucephalus; 7. Black Bess; 8. Barb; 9. Blackberry; 10. Babieca.

HORSE WORDS.

The little girls ran to join their friends at the picnic, just as a man from the brewery was making an announcement to everyone. "Ladies and gentlemen, boys and girls," he said. "I'm delighted to welcome you all here once again, and I hope that this year's picnic will be a great success. We've plenty of fun and games lined up for you all, so let's get off to a good start with our usual three-legged race. Take your partners, please!"

There was a great deal of laughing and joking as all the competitors lined up for the start of the race. Alice had teamed up with a little boy called Paul, who lived quite near the Rose and Crown.

"On your marks, get set, go!" cried the starter, and the race began. It was a close thing, with many tumbles and false starts, but as the runners neared the finishing line, Mr and Mrs Atkins were delighted to see Alice and Paul overtaking everyone else, to finish in first place.

It was a wonderful start to the day, and Alice joined in game after game, spurred on by her success. Mr and Mrs Atkins had wondered if a whole day out might be too tiring for her, but from the happy look on her face they could see that they need not have worried. From time to time she would run over to where the horses were quietly resting, and stroke Black Beauty's nose, and then she would race back to the picnic, to be sure she didn't miss any of the fun.

Then the man from the brewery made another announcement: "Gather round, children," he began, "and form into groups. It's time for the nature ramble along the river bank. Stay close together and watch out for slippy patches. We don't want anyone falling in!"

Everybody laughed as the children formed into small groups, and each group set off in the direction of the river. Alice was in the last group, and Mr and Mrs Atkins decided that they would tag along behind, just to keep an eye on her.

The children loved the river, and they eagerly pointed to the small brown trout which darted among the rocks, and the shoals of silvery, striped minnows which swam alongside the banks. There were a hundred and one interesting things to look at in the river, and all the children clustered round the banks, jostling each other for the best places.

And then a terrible thing happened. One particular group of children were pushing each other even harder than the rest, and suddenly there was a loud *splash*, and a little girl's scream, as one of the children fell in.

Mr and Mrs Atkins watched in horror, and Mr Atkins leapt forward to see if he could rescue the child. At first, neither of them could see clearly through the group of children, but suddenly both of them caught their breath as they saw who the child was. It was Alice, and she was crying and screaming as the current carried her down the river.

Mr Atkins set off down the bank, calling out to her not to panic, and he tried desperately to get ahead of her on the bank, so that he could dive in and save her. But the current was strong, and Alice was being swept along at a terrible speed.

Suddenly he turned his head, as he heard an unmistakable sound behind him. It was the sound of thundering hooves. Then came another sound – a loud whinny – as Black Beauty caught up with Jack Atkins and slowed down to a walk.

"I don't know how you managed to get here, Beauty," cried Jack, as he flung himself up onto Beauty's back, "but I'm glad to see you!"

Beauty set off at speed again along the bank, whinnying loudly, and Mr Atkins had to cling on tightly to his mane. Within seconds they were ahead of Alice, and it was time for Mr Atkins to jump down from the horse's back and plunge

into the water. Just seconds later, the current swept Alice into his outstretched arms.

As he grabbed her, Mr Atkins watched her face anxiously. All the time he had been racing along the bank, the thought had been going through his mind that a shock like this could put Alice so far back in her progress that she would take to her bed again. He was desperately worried, but as he looked at her he was astonished to see a smile on her face.

"You're safe now, Alice," he said gently, as he pulled her out of the water, where Mrs Atkins was just arriving with a warm coat to put on the child. "Were you very frightened?"

"I was at first, father," she said, "but then I saw that you were running after me, and I heard Black Beauty's whinnying. I just *knew* I'd be safe then."

They sat Alice on Beauty's back, and the fine stallion walked steadily back to the picnic, where a great cheer went up to celebrate the brave rescue.

"What you've got there, Charlie," said Jack Atkins, as he stroked Black Beauty's nose and Alice looked down happily, "is a horse in a million. Worth his weight in gold, ten times over."

"I know," smiled Charlie Dixon. "I'm proud of him."

Tee~Hee Haw

Bovril, jam or peanut butter with bananas?

At least he shouldn't have any trouble making the weight.